Contents

What is a lake?

A lake is a large body of fresh or salty water that lies inland. Its waters are never connected directly to the sea. Some lakes lie high up in the mountains. Other lakes are low lying. But all of them are fed by rain, springs, streams or rivers. The water in lakes is never completely still. We shall see how the Earth's **water cycle** affects the lakes of the world.

Lake Titicaca is the largest lake in South America. The lake is the highest **navigable** lake in the world, lying 3811 m above sea level. The great Incan civilization was built around the lake shores.

Lakes

Catherine Chambers

Heinemann
LIBRARY

First published in Great Britain by Heinemann Library,
Halley Court, Jordan Hill, Oxford OX2 8EJ,
a division of Reed Educational and Professional Publishing Ltd.
Heinemann is a registered trademark of Reed Educational & Professional Publishing Limited.

OXFORD MELBOURNE AUCKLAND
JOHANNESBURG BLANTYRE GABORONE
IBADAN PORTSMOUTH NH (USA) CHICAGO

© Reed Educational and Professional Publishing Ltd 2001
The moral right of the proprietor has been asserted.

Designed by David Oakley
Illustrations by Tokay Interactive Ltd
Originated by Dot Gradations
Printed in Hong Kong/China

05 04 03 02 01
10 9 8 7 6 5 4 3 2 1

ISBN 0 431 09849 2
This title is also available in a hardback library edition (ISBN 0 431 09842 5)

British Library Cataloguing in Publication Data

Chambers, Catherine
        Lakes. – (Mapping earthforms)
        1. Lake ecology – Juvenile literature 2. Lakes – Maps –
        Juvenile literature
        I. Title
        577.6'3

Acknowledgements
The Publishers would like to thank the following for permission to reproduce photographs: Aspect Picture
Library Ltd: T Okuda p5; Bruce Coleman Limited: B and C Calhoun p17, Dr M Kahl p18, R Meier p19; Corbis:
p14; Ecoscene: S Donachie p26; Robert Harding Picture Library: p8, R Francis p20; Oxford Scientific Films: p24,
B Littlehales p9, C Milkins p16, S Osolinski p12; Panos Pictures: H Bradman p25; Still Pictures: E Cleigne p15,
Paul Harrison p4, R Seitres p7, J Wark p10, H Schwarzbach p23, Eastlight p29.

Cover photograph reproduced with permission of Robert MacKinlay and Still Pictures.

Every effort has been made to contact copyright holders of any material reproduced in this book. Any
omissions will be rectified in subsequent printings if notice is given to the Publisher.

For more information about Heinemann Library books, or to order, please phone ++44 (0)1865 888066, or send
a fax to ++44 (0)1865 314091. You can visit our website at www.heinemann.co.uk.

Any words appearing in the text in bold, **like this**, are explained in the Glossary.

How have lakes formed?

Lakes have formed in many different ways. Some have been formed by great tongues of compressed snow **scouring** out hollows in the Earth's surface. Other lakes occur in dips at the bottom of folds in masses of rock – or in **extinct** volcanoes. Lakes are also formed when valleys are blocked by **landslides**. Some lakes fill huge cracks or **faults** made when the Earth's crust moves. Others are formed where rivers cross flat valley floors. You can discover more about how lakes were formed and filled on pages 10 and 11.

Lake Biwa is Japan's biggest lake. It is an important waterway, connected to the Kamogawa **Canal**. It also provides power to the bustling city of Kyoto. But more than this, Lake Biwa is beautiful and a sacred lake for Japanese people. It has had many poems written about it and features in Japanese legends.

What do lakes look like?

Lakes can be very small. Many small lakes are found high in the mountains or very low down on river **flood plains.** Others are long and thin. These are known as ribbon lakes. Many of them lie in huge cracks in the Earth's crust. Other lakes are vast inland seas. We shall see how lakes fill different shapes, and how manmade ones have altered the landscape around them. We will also see that lakes are changing all the time.

Life in and around lakes

Many fresh-water lakes are full of plant and animal life. They attract humans too. But some lakes have very little life in and around them. Salt-water lakes often teem with fish. But in very salty lakes there is very little visible life. We shall see why some lakes attract living things and what the future holds for the lakes of the world.

The lakes of the world

Lakes occur all over the world. They range from huge lakes called seas to small lakes on islands. Some lakes lie in cool, wet areas; others lie in hot, dry areas. Many lakes are found high up in rocky mountains or on **plateaux**, while some are found low down on flat **plains**. Lakes are always changing. They can fill up **basins** in wet months of the year and then disappear in hot, dry weather. Some lakes disappear altogether over a long time.

 You can see from the map that lakes can occur in hot, quite dry areas as well as cool, wet ones. In deserts like the Sahara and the Great Australian Desert there are huge underground lakes that you cannot see.

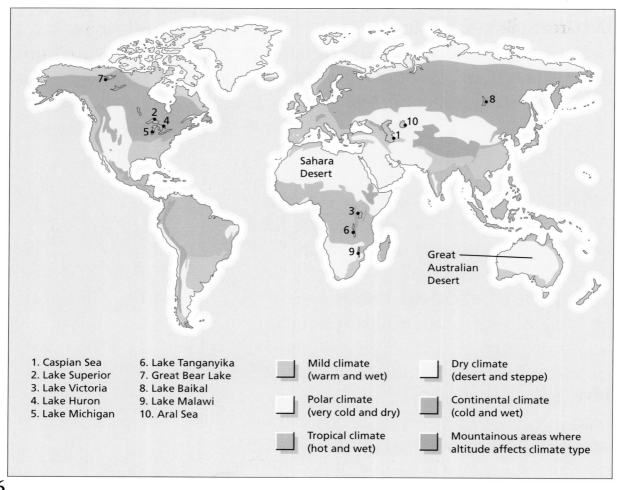

Sahara Desert

Great Australian Desert

1. Caspian Sea
2. Lake Superior
3. Lake Victoria
4. Lake Huron
5. Lake Michigan
6. Lake Tanganyika
7. Great Bear Lake
8. Lake Baikal
9. Lake Malawi
10. Aral Sea

Mild climate (warm and wet)

Polar climate (very cold and dry)

Tropical climate (hot and wet)

Dry climate (desert and steppe)

Continental climate (cold and wet)

Mountainous areas where altitude affects climate type

Large lakes and little lakes

The biggest lakes are found on huge land masses called **continents**. The Caspian Sea is the largest salt-water lake in the world. It lies between eastern Europe and central Asia. Lake Superior is the largest fresh-water lake in the world. It is found on the continent of North America, where half of the world's lakes lie.

Small lakes can be found high up in mountains. Small mountain lakes are called **tarns**.

Groups of lakes

If you look at the world map you will see that in some places there are groups of lakes. In North America, five large lakes make up a group called the Great Lakes. In northern Europe, the country of Finland has lakes all over it. There are more than 60,000 of them! Some of these are very small. The Great Lakes and the lakes of Finland were made by ice **eroding** massive areas of land.

Lake Eyre is the biggest lake on the continent of Australia. It was once part of a huge inland sea. It covers 9300 sq km (3600 sq mi). But it is also the world's largest temporary lake. For if there is very little rain for a few years, the lake completely disappears.

Another group of lakes lies on the eastern side of Africa. This group includes Lake Victoria – the second-largest fresh-water lake in the world. The east African lakes formed in a huge crack that ripped the Earth's surface millions of years ago. This crack is known as the Rift Valley.

Lake landscapes

There are countless different lake shapes: ranging from tiny mountain **tarns** to huge inland seas; from long, thin ribbon lakes to round **crater** lakes. Lake landscapes vary from rolling green hills to bare, rocky **gorges**. Lakes and their landscapes are changing all the time. Some of these changes are natural and others are caused by humans.

A changing landscape

Some lake landscapes change during a single year. This is because they lie where there is a very dry season and a very rainy one. Lake Chad in central Africa is an example of this. Some lakes are so large that they have different landscapes in different parts of the lake. Lake Tiberius is also known as the Sea of Galilee. It lies in the Rift Valley in Jordan.

Morning mists are a common feature of lake landscapes. When the night skies are clear, the moist air above the lake often gets very cold. The water droplets in the cold air turn into mist or fog clouds, which you can see early in the morning. When the sun comes out, the warmed air rises from the lake and the water droplets **evaporate.** The mist disappears.

The lake is completely surrounded by beaches. But in the north and north-west there are flat **plains.** In the east and south-west there are cliffs.

Some lakes have sandy shores, while others have banks and flats of mud. Many lakes have marshlands around their edges. This happens where the lake is slowly being filled with fine soil, called **silt.**

Clear lakes and blue lakes

The waters of Lake Tiberius are cool and clear. But some lakes are so deep that you cannot see into the water at all. Other lakes are bright blue. Sometimes this is because the water acts like a mirror so that it reflects the blue sky. At other times it is caused by **minerals** in the water. Crater lakes, which form in **extinct** volcanoes, are often like this. A good example of a chemically-blue lake is Crater Lake in the USA.

Crater Lake in Oregon, USA, was formed in an extinct volcano. When it rains, water runs down the steep sides of the crater and into the hole. Water seeps away into the rock. It also **evaporates** into the air when the sun is hot. The moisture becomes **water vapour** and is carried away from the volcano and into the air. The lake is famous for the changing colours of its waters — especially for its beautiful blue.

How lakes are formed

The moving Earth

Many lakes fill great splits in large masses of rock. These splits, or **faults,** are caused by movements deep down in the Earth's crust. The Rift Valley in eastern Africa is an example of this.

Other lakes have formed in dips made when the Earth's surface crumpled into folds. These folds are made up of layers of different types of rock. Lakes occur when a dip is made of a layer of rock that will not soak up the water that runs into it. This kind of rock is known as **impermeable**.

These are oxbow or cutoff lakes. These lakes form gradually as a river carves loops in its channel. The curve of the loop gets rounder while the neck of the loop shrinks. Then the waters of the river force themselves over the neck, cutting off the loop. In the end, most oxbow lakes become boggy and shrink to nothing.

Lakes are also formed when rock **landslides** block the ends of valleys. Valleys are carved out by the action of streams, rivers or ice.

The power of ice

The power of moving ice has formed many of the world's biggest lakes, which are called glacial lakes. They are formed by huge tongues of ice, called **glaciers.** These glaciers are pulled down mountains by the force of **gravity.** As they slip down the slope they **scour** out great valleys in the rock. They carry bits of broken rock with them. When the ice finally melts, the rocks get dumped, or deposited, at the ends of valleys. This blocks the valleys, which are then filled with water. Long, thin glacial lakes are called ribbon lakes.

High up in mountain ranges, glaciers scour out smaller dips. They leave a lip of rock at the edge, so water gets trapped in the dip. These lakes are called **tarns**. Many of today's glacial lake **basins** were formed during the last **Ice Age**. This began to retreat about 10,000 years ago, allowing the basins to fill with water.

Underground lakes

You cannot see all the lakes of the world. Some lie underground. Water seeps through soil and soaks through rock on the surface. Then it reaches an impermeable basin underneath. The water cannot soak through the basin so it just sits on top of it. A large part of Australia lies over a huge underground lake.

The Great Lakes

The five Great Lakes of North America together make up the largest body of fresh-water in the world. They include Lake Superior, the world's biggest fresh-water lake. The other Great Lakes are Ontario, Erie, Huron and Michigan. If you look at the map you can see that they cover a huge area of North America. You can also see how humans have connected the lakes together by building **canals.**

Making and shaping

Many lakes were formed by one action and then reshaped over time by different actions. The Great Lakes are a good example of this. Lake Superior lies in what

The Great Lakes have some breathtaking scenery. Here you can see the Pictured Rocks, which lie on the south-east shore of Lake Superior. The rocks are multicoloured sandstone cliffs. But the lakes are also rich in wood and **minerals** such as iron, copper and silver. This has meant that a lot of mines and factories have been built along the lake shores.

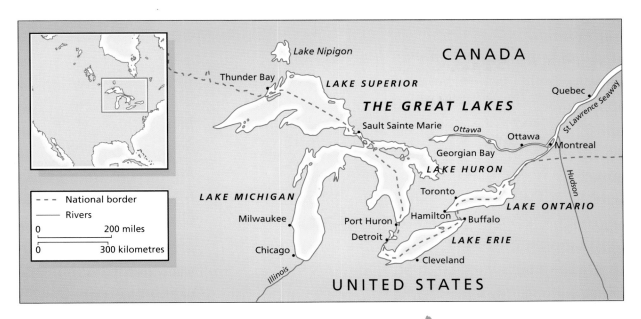

Lake Nipigon · Thunder Bay · **LAKE SUPERIOR** · **THE GREAT LAKES** · Sault Sainte Marie · Ottawa · Ottawa · Georgian Bay · **LAKE HURON** · Toronto · **LAKE MICHIGAN** · Milwaukee · Port Huron · Hamilton · Buffalo · **LAKE ONTARIO** · Detroit · **LAKE ERIE** · Chicago · Cleveland · Illinois · **CANADA** · Quebec · St Lawrence Seaway · Montreal · Hudson · **UNITED STATES**

- - - National border
—— Rivers

0   200 miles
0   300 kilometres

was once just a wide valley. To the south-east were low-lying **plains**. Then, in the last **Ice Age**, great tongues of compressed snow deepened the valley and gouged out huge holes in the plains. The valley and plains filled with water and formed the Great Lakes.

Then, the lake beds were changed yet again. Over 10,000 years ago, a movement in the Earth's crust lifted up the northern end of the lakes. This caused the water to tip into the Saint Lawrence Seaway, which it does to this day.

The lakes are fed by rivers and streams. The Great Lakes' waters are also increased by melting snow and ice, called **meltwater**. The lakes higher up feed into the lakes lower down, through rivers. Lake Superior, for example, drains into Lake Huron.

The lakes have huge bays in places. Some of the lakes have islands that are large enough for people to live on them.

The Great Lakes have been made into one of the world's biggest shipping **networks**. Canals have been dug between the lakes where the rivers are too shallow or dangerous for boats. In 1959 the Saint Lawrence Seaway Project connected the lakes to the Atlantic Ocean with a deep canal, used by medium-sized ocean-going ships. The lakes are also connected to the Mexican Gulf through the Illinois Waterway and the Mississippi River. But during the harsh winters, the lakes freeze and shipping stops.

13

Lake waters

Lake waters rise and fall all the time. Some dry up completely during the hot, dry months of the year. They fill up again during cooler, wetter months. Over many years, lakes grow or shrink and change their shape. Some turn into marshland, while others turn to dust.

Most lake waters are fed by rivers, streams and melting snow and ice. Some are fed by underground springs. A small amount of water comes from raindrops falling on the lake's surface. But however they are fed, lake waters are always on the move.

Lake Erie is one of the Great Lakes of North America (see pages 12–13). It looks calm here, at Detroit, USA, but its waters are quite shallow. This means that in stormy weather, huge swells of water rise from the bottom, causing large waves on the surface. It can be quite dangerous for ships, especially in winter when the storms are very fierce.

Moving waters

Strong winds whip lake waters into waves. But lake waters also move underneath the surface. Rivers and streams pour their cold waters into the warmer top layer of lake water. The cold water sinks, because it is heavier than the warm water above it. The cold water mixes and moves the water already there. This is called a current, and is like the currents that flow in seas and oceans.

In the hot summer months, a lake has a layer of warm water which rests on top of a cold layer. In the autumn, the top layer of water cools and sinks. It mixes with the water underneath and causes movement. This disturbs the lake's surface with little choppy waves.

Lake waters can also move very slowly around the lake's **basin**, like soup swirling around a bowl. These movements are called **seiches.** Some seiches are caused by strong winds. But most happen because of the Earth's constant rotation.

Lake Chad lies in central Africa. In the wet season the waters cover 25,900 sq km (10,000 sq mi). But in the dry season they shrink to less than half that size. In the north-west, the lake is only about 1 m deep. In the south it is about 6 m deep. Lake Chad is getting smaller all the time. This is partly because the hotter **climate** is causing more water to **evaporate** into the air. But water is also seeping through the rock in the lake basin.

15

Lake plants

Still or slow-moving fresh-water lakes provide a rich **habitat** for a wide range of plants – from tiny **algae** to large flowering waterlilies. Many types of grassy reed and rush grow on marshy lake edges. This is known as a **lentic** habitat.

Leafy lake plants

Most leafy lake plants have waxy leaves and thick stems which protect them from the water. They also hold the leaves above the water's surface. Some leaves are flat and floating, like rafts. The main roots of lake plants reach far down into the **silt** at the bottom of the lake. There are sometimes also very fine, feathery roots, called **tendrils**, that dangle from the stem. These absorb **minerals** from the water around them. The roots of lake plants take

Water plants and creatures need oxygen in the water to survive. Lake plants make oxygen when the sun acts on the green cells in their leaves. The elodea crispa, found in many parts of the world, is especially good at this. It has long spikey stems with scores of bright green, thin, curled leaves. Bubbles of oxygen rise from tiny holes in each leaf. Elodea crispa is now grown and sold to people who have ponds or goldfish tanks. The plant gives fish and other creatures oxygen. It also helps to keep still water clean.

in a large amount of water. But a lot of the moisture **evaporates** through thousands of tiny holes in the plants' leaves. Without the holes, the plants would rot.

Tiny algae

But some fresh-water lakes contain very few plants. These lakes often have crystal-clear water – you can see right down to the bottom. The edges of the lake are rocky, with no soil in which waterside plants can grow. But in the summer, you might see a thin, milky film on the surface of the water. This is made by millions of very tiny plants known as algae, which grow when the sun warms the water. Some algae grow even in the coldest water. An orange-pink algae grows in the lakes of Antarctica. Other kinds of algae also grow in salt-water lakes. But the Dead Sea has water that is so salty that no real plants can grow in it at all.

The white waterlily can grow in water up to 3 m deep and thrives in many parts of Europe. Its long, strong stems carry large, round, flat leaves that float on the surface. The cup-shaped flowers float too. The lily's flask-shaped seed pods ripen underwater. When they burst, the seeds float on the surface, which carries them far and wide. The very thick bottom part of the waterlily's stem is called a rhyzome. Long ago, people in northern Europe used it as food.

Creatures of the lakes

In both salt-water and fresh-water lakes, creatures have adapted their bodies and habits to living in and around the water. The lakes are home to many species of **mammal, reptile, amphibian,** bird and fish. But in crystal-clear fresh-water lakes, there are very few creatures. In the very salty waters of the Dead Sea, no creature, not even fish, can survive for long.

Life in the lake

Many fresh-water lake creatures are the same as those living in rivers and streams.

 Pink flamingoes flock in their thousands to Lake Naivasha in east Africa. The bird's long, curved bill scoops up tiny shellfish from the muddy water. The flamingo's pink colour comes from its diet of shellfish. Its webbed feet enable it to stand on the soft mud. Its long legs keep its feathers well above the water. The flamingo nests on mudflats or heaps of mud above the lake's surface.

But the Lake Baikal seal in Siberia is the only fresh-water seal in the world. Its thick layers of fat help it to cope with the freezing waters during the harsh winters.

In hot east and central Africa, the hippopotamus thrives in large lakes. During the day it can travel 40 kilometres (25 miles), eating water plants as it goes. Only its eyes, ears and nostrils can be seen as it swims along. But the hippopotamus is able to swim underwater for five minutes too. Flaps in its nostrils close as it enters the water.

Amphibians live half in the water and half out of it. The adults breathe air. But their young **larvae** are **hatched** in the water and breathe through gills. Lakes are a good **habitat** for many types of amphibious frog, toad and newt.

The fresh-water pike fish hides at the shallow edges of large lakes where there are a lot of water plants. It uses its powerful body to dart forward and catch its prey. The pike's huge mouth and sharp teeth quickly snap around passing fish. The powan and the vendace are two small fish that live in mountain lakes in northern Europe. They have adapted to swallowing tiny creatures called **plankton** that float in the water.

This terrapin lives in south and central Europe. It is a reptile, so it breathes air on land, but often feeds in the water. The terrapin likes to live near quite still waters, so it often chooses lakes. It dives in the water when it is disturbed and swims with its strong back legs. A tough shell protects it from other meat-eating creatures. The terrapin eats fish, amphibians and sometimes small land creatures. It has no teeth but catches its prey with a horny beak.

Peoples of the lakes

All over the world people have settled near lakes. For thousands of years these settlers have used lake waters for drinking, cooking, washing and growing crops. Lakes have provided people with meat and fish to eat. Trees and reeds surrounding the lakes have given materials for building homes, boats, baskets and matting.

In more recent times, **minerals** such as iron, copper and silver have been mined around lakes. Petroleum oil has also been found in places. These natural riches have provided jobs which have attracted many people to the lakes. Ports grew as more farm products, minerals and manufactured goods were transported across the waters. Towns and even great cities have risen around these ports.

◆ Chicago rests on low-lying ground by Lake Michigan — one of the Great Lakes in the United States. About 170 years ago, Chicago was a lake settlement with just twelve families. Today it is one of the biggest inland ports in the world. The Great Lakes are surrounded by huge farmlands, allowing the city to develop as a centre for the meat and cereal trade. Then Chicago's expansion continued as industry grew.

Homes in the lakes

Thousands of years ago people made their homes in the lakes. This provided protection against enemies and rising lake waters. In quiet lake waters, buildings rested on short wooden stumps called piles. The piles were stuck into mounds of mud or terraces of stone. Stone walls were built around the mud mounds and stone terraces to stop them from falling apart.

Stone Age builders in Wangen, Switzerland, made huge settlements. Over 50,000 long piles were used to hold them up. Later, in the Bronze Age, even bigger settlements were made, with two-storey buildings. These ancient peoples traded leather goods, textiles and pottery. Today some communities still make homes in the lake waters. South Americans build houses in lakes near the Orinoco and Amazon Rivers.

Lake Michigan has enabled Chicago to become the largest city in the Great Lakes area. This map shows how roads fan out to other towns in the region and suburbs stretch along the lake shore.

A way of life – the Luo of Lake Victoria

Lake Victoria lies in east Africa. It is the second-largest fresh-water lake in the world. The Luo people began to settle on its eastern shores over 500 years ago. Before that they lived further north in Sudan. Here, they herded cattle on open grassland. But Lake Victoria had everything that they wanted – good pasture for their cattle and lots of fish. They could buy cereals grown by the Gusii people on the fertile hillsides nearby. As well as this there was a constant supply of materials for building. Many Luo still use the natural lake environment to make a living and build a home.

This map shows where most Luo settlements lie near Lake Victoria. It also shows the port of Kisumu and the fertile hills around the lake.

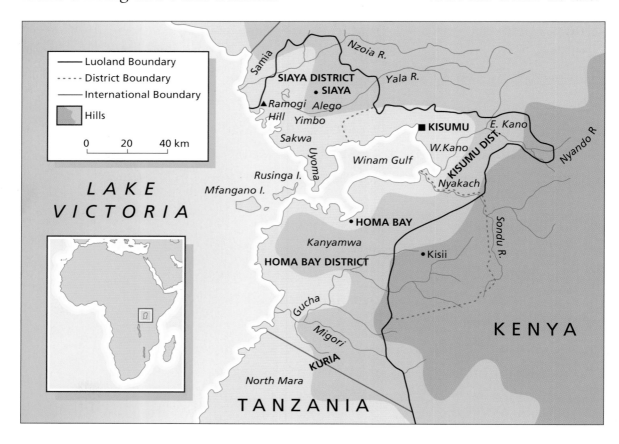

Making a living

Today, many fishermen still use slender, wooden canoes to go fishing. They catch mostly long lungfish and fat, meaty tilapia (fresh-water fish found in Africa). Traditionally, some of these were preserved by smoking or drying them. The Luo fishermen now mostly use modern nets to catch the fish. But some still set traps, which are long baskets made of dried reeds.

Today, Luo farmers grow cash crops for export, as well as keeping animals. Many people work in transport, industry and commerce in the lake port of Kisumu.

Building a home

The muddy lake shores provide good material for building lakeside homes. Some houses are still built in the traditional way. Wet clay is daubed on a circular framework of poles. The roof is also made of poles tied in a cone shape and thatched with reeds or cereal stalks. Clay is also used to make pots. Reeds and stalks are woven into baskets.

Large boats carry goods to all parts of Lake Victoria from the city port of Kisumu. Kisumu is also linked to Kenya's coastal port, Mombasa, by a railway line. Nearly a hundred years ago, Kisumu exported animal skins, wild rubber, beeswax and other natural products. Today, cotton, coffee and manufactured goods are transported across the waters. But Lake Victoria is changing. The spread of water hyacinth has led to small harbours becoming blocked.

Our changing lakes

Natural changes?

Lakes change all the time. Some lakes get deeper as more ice and snow melt into them. Others get shallower as the waters **evaporate** or seep through the rock beneath. Over time, some fill up with fine soil called **silt**. Many lake edges turn into marshland full of reeds and waterweeds. Some lakes end up as wetlands covered in grass and wild flowers. Others are left as **basins** of dry rock.

In recent years lakes have evaporated more quickly. This is because of general changes in the Earth's **climate**. No one is sure if this is a natural change or not. Some scientists think that the hotter weather is caused by temporary changes in the heat coming from the Sun. Other scientists think that it is because a layer of gases in

The River Volga runs down into the world's biggest salt-water lake — the Caspian Sea. About 40 years ago, strings of manmade lakes were made along the river. This meant that 80 per cent less water flowed into the lake. Many scientists thought that the dams alone were responsible for drying it up. But ancient Islamic records showed that the water level lowers naturally every 70 years.

the atmosphere around the Earth is getting thinner. This is called the **ozone layer** and it protects the Earth from the sun's rays. These scientists also believe that humans are making the ozone layer thinner by letting too many harmful gases called CFCs into the atmosphere. And

perhaps burning fossil fuels such as oil and coal is releasing too many carbon gases – causing global warming. But we do not really know.

Life in the lakes changes as waters get shallower and more polluted. There are fewer plants and animals. Natural life is also damaged by polluted rain, called **acid rain**. It kills the tiny **algae** that form in lakes during the summer months.

Manmade changes

In some places lake waters are getting shallower because we are stopping rivers from flowing into them. Rivers are blocked to control flooding or so that the waters can flow into artificial lakes called **dams.** These are often made by flooding valleys. When this happens, people have to move out of their homes and natural **habitats** are destroyed. The dams are used to **irrigate** areas of dry farmland. Dams are also built to provide hydro-electric power (HEP) for large city populations and industry.

When the waters of the Caspian Sea got lower, the land on the lake shores got bigger. Farmers began to grow crops on it. Factories and a nuclear power station were built. But the fishing waters became more polluted. The dams on the River Volga also stopped sturgeon fish from swimming up from the lake to lay their eggs in the river.

Looking to the future

Our lakes are very useful, busy places. They are beautiful too. But can nature and humans both thrive together in and around them? We want a lot of things from our lakes. We want the creatures and plant life to stay as they are. But the beauty of lakes and water sports also attract a lot of tourists to their shores. Tourists have meant more pollution, and many hotels have been built along the lake shores. Both of these destroy the natural beauty that we enjoy so much.

We use lakes for transport and to provide jobs. The shores are good places to build factories, which often need water for manufacturing. Factories use the waters to carry away their waste too. Lakeside forests

Lake Baikal formed in a split, or rift, in the Earth's surface 25 million years ago. It has over 1500 of its own species of plant and animal. The lake can tell us a lot about how life on Earth has changed. This is why it is so important to keep the waters clean and to preserve the plants and creatures in it.

Map labels:

R U S S I A

Nizhneangarsk

Tulun

Lim

Lene

Zima

Balagansk

Kachug

Lake Baikal

Oka

Zalan

Kutulik

Cheremkhovo

Barguzip

Vitim

Usol'ye-Sibirskoye

Ust'Ordynskiy

B U R Y A T I A

Angarsk **Irkutsk**

Uda

Chita

Kyren

Babushkin Ulan-Ude

Ingoda

Petrovsk-Zabaykal'skiy

provide trees which are felled and floated along the lake to sawmills built around the shores. **Minerals** are mined in and around lakes.

The best of both worlds

The story of Lake Baikal shows just how nature and human activity can thrive side by side. Lake Baikal lies in southern Siberia, in Russia. It is the world's oldest and deepest lake. In winter and spring the lake is covered in a thick layer of ice. In the summer and autumn it is crystal clear. This is because billions of shrimps eat up the tiny **algae** plants and **bacteria** in the water. But Lake Baikal's clear waters made it a good place for making high-quality plastics, paper and cardboard using the surrounding trees. The factories polluted the waters badly. So, in 1987, they were forced to find other ways of getting rid of their solid waste. They could no longer pump harmful chemicals into the water either. Now, the waters are clear again.

The shape of Lake Baikal shows us that it has formed in a split in the Earth's crust. Many rivers flow into and out of the lake, so any pollution affects a wider area than just the lake.

Lake facts

The top ten lakes

These are the top ten lakes of the world. Some of the lakes are called seas. But they are really lakes because they are large bodies of water surrounded by land. The table shows the lakes in order of the area of water they normally hold. But lakes change all the time, so it is a very difficult figure to calculate and gets quickly out of date.

	Continent	Area (sq km)	Area (sq mi)
Caspian Sea	Asia/Europe	371,800	143,550
Lake Superior	North America	82,350	31,800
Lake Victoria	Africa	68,000	26,000
Lake Huron	North America	59,600	23,010
Lake Michigan	North America	58,000	22,400
Aral Sea	Asia	36,000	13,900
Lake Tanganyika	Africa	33,000	13,000
Great Bear Lake	North America	31,800	12,280
Lake Baikal	Asia	30,500	11,780
Lake Malawi/Nyasa	Africa	29,600	11,430

Highest, lowest, deepest

The highest lake: Lake Titicaca, which is 3811 m above sea level.

The lowest lake: The Dead Sea, which is 403 m below sea level.

The deepest lake: Lake Baikal, which reaches down 1940 m (1485 m below sea level).

The Aral Sea lies in central Asia. It was once the fourth-biggest lake in the world. But its waters have been heavily used for **irrigation**. They have dropped by over half in the last 40 years. The water level is now so low that the lake has divided into two.

Glossary

acid rain rain-water that has been polluted by chemicals. It is caused by gases released into the air from factories and motor vehicles.

algae simple form of plant life, ranging from a single cell to a huge seaweed

amphibian animal, with a backbone, that develops in water and can stay in the water for long periods, but can also live on land. Frogs, toads and newts are amphibians.

bacteria tiny, one-celled organisms, some of which can cause disease

basin lake floor – shaped like a washbasin. It can also mean the area of land around a river and its tributaries.

canal manmade waterway, rather like a river, built for boats and ships

climate rainfall, temperature and winds that normally affect a large area

continent the world's largest land masses. Continents are usually divided into many countries.

crater hole or hollow in the top of a volcano

dam wall that is built across a river valley to hold back water, creating an artificial lake

erosion wearing away of rocks and soil by wind, water, ice or acid

evaporate turn from solid or liquid into vapour, such as water becoming water vapour

extinct dead – no longer active

fault crack deep in the Earth's crust

flood plain flat land in a valley bottom that is regularly flooded

glacier thick mass of ice formed from compressed snow. Glaciers flow downhill.

gorge narrow river valley with very steep sides

gravity force that causes objects to fall towards the Earth. We are all attracted to the Earth by gravity.

habitat place where a plant or animal usually grows or lives

hatch when a young creature is born by bursting out of its egg

Ice Age time when snow and ice covered much of the Earth

impermeable substance that does not allow water to pass through it

irrigate supply a place or area with water, for example to grow crops

landslide when the top surface of soil and rock slips down a slope

larva(e) the undeveloped but active young of creatures such as insects and frogs

lentic slow-moving water habitat for creatures and plants

mammal animal that feeds its young with its own milk

meltwater water that has melted from ice and snow

mineral substance that is formed naturally in rocks and earth, such as coal, tin or salt

navigable waterways that are deep and wide enough for ships to use them

network system with lots of connected lines, passages and so on

ozone layer layer of gases, high up in the Earth's atmosphere, that protects us from the sun's harmful rays

plain area of flat land or low-lying hills

plankton tiny water creatures that can be either plants or animals

plateau area of high, flat ground, often lying between mountains

reptile cold-blooded, egg-laying animal with a spine and a scaly skin, such as a crocodile

scour rub hard against something, wearing it away

seich slow movement of lake waters around their basins

silt fine particles of eroded rock and soil that can settle in lakes and rivers, sometimes blocking the movement of water

tarn small mountain lake eroded by a glacier

tendril fine, feathery root

water cycle the system by which the Earth's water is constantly changing, from rivers, lakes and seas to water vapour in the air, which falls as rain on to the ground and drains into rivers, lakes and seas again

water vapour water that has been heated so much that it forms a gas which is held in the air – drops of water form again when the vapour is cooled. There is always water vapour present in the air.

Index